FROM NEW RELEASE TO BESTSELLER

PLAYBOOK FOR THE ASPIRING AUTHOR WHO IS
READY TO GET PAID!

———

CHARRON MONAYE

Published By: Pen Legacy®

Cover Edited & Formatting By: Tamika Hall

Library of Congress Cataloging – in- Publication Data has been applied for.

ISBN #: 9798986073217

PRINTED IN THE UNITED STATES OF AMERICA

Why Charron Monaye?

When Charron Monaye embarked on her journey to become an entrepreneur and author, she was broke, had no business knowledge, and was so clueless regarding marketing that she couldn't even sell a pen. The only thing she possessed was a composition book of poetry and a desire to share her story, hoping to sell enough books to provide for her children.

She believed having a published book would wipe away her debt and solve her financial troubles, but that myth was soon debunked. Even after finally getting her first book published, she had no business or marketing plan, no clear understanding of her target audience, no selling system, and no team. She was a one-woman show, and without being financially able to hire a coach or build a team, she struggled from 2008 to 2014. She not only suffered physically from the stress, but her lack of knowledge and planning cost her tons of money, time, and freedom as a result of repeated losses and unlearned lessons.

In 2014, she decided to use her savings to invest in herself – hiring a coach, paying for mastermind classes, and studying the strategies of others who were already winning. She went from being broken and broke to building businesses, attracting clients, selling thousands of books, and being recognized in the industry as a literary game-changer. It's okay to have a desire to tell your story and self-publish by uploading your book, but what's not okay is failing to plan. If you don't have a plan, process, or strategy, you will lose money, get in debt, receive no returns from your investment, and have no sales.

If you are ready to go from being a new author to being a blazing bestseller, then working with Charron Monaye is the answer. Below are some of her most honorable accomplishments.

1992

- Contributed to the book anthology Tears of Fire: The National Library of Poetry

1995

- Contributed to the book anthology Best Poems of 1995: The National Library of Poetry

2008

- December 5, 2008 - Started writing journey under the name Pen Legacy at Kandi Burrus's event in Atlanta, GA.
- Secured the position of Staff Writer of The Philadelphia Forum, under The Philadelphia Association of Paralegals

2011

- Wrote lyrics for ML The Truth's song "Commitment", which was later considered for a Grammy Award in the category Best R&B Song.
- Contributed to the Book Anthologies: A Poetically Spoken Anthology, Vol. 1 and Voices Behind The Tears
- Became a published author; *My Side of the Story* released under Purposeful Publishing.

2012

- Became a Journalist and Contributing Columnist for CNN iReport
- Recognized as Outstanding Contribution to Poetry by Great Poets Across America

- Contributed to book anthologies The Homeless Cry and Stars in Our Hearts: Diversity
- Wrote and co-produced first theatrical production, *Living Your Life.*
- Released second book, *Living, Loving, & Laughing My Way Through under Purposeful Publishing.*

2013

- Honored in Cleveland, OH by the organization Girls on Fire; received the Presidential Award and Best Independent Author Award.
- Wrote and produced theatrical production, *Why Can't We Be Friends, an anti-bullying play.*

2014

- *Why Can't We Be Friends*, an anti-bullying play, won Best Real-Life Drama Stage Play at the Playwright Awards in Queens, NY.

2015

- Released & became an Amazon Best-Selling Author with third release, *Love the Real You,* published under Pen Legacy Publishing.
- Pen Legacy Publishing officially opened for business on May 10th.

2016

- Released & became an Amazon Best-Selling Author with fourth release, *STOP Asking for Permission & Give Notice.*
- Hired to write two theatrical productions, *Oliva Lost & Turned Out* and *Til Death Do U Part.*

2017

- Named "Woman Who Is Doing It Big" at Millionaire Mogul, Tiana Von Johnson's Women Doing It Big Conference in New York City.
- Co-authored memoirs by Neo-Soul Singer/Songwriter Jaguar Wright and Philadelphia Police Officer Deborah Rose.
- Hired to write two theatrical productions, *Testify* and *Cheatin' In the Next Room.*
- Pen Legacy officially registered as a Limited Liability Corporation in the Commonwealth of Pennsylvania.
- Participated in the Literary Takeover Book Signing in New Orleans, LA, during Essence Festival.
- Studied "Writing for Television" under television producer, screenwriter, and author Shonda Rhimes.
- Received professional recognition and endorsement from Word of Life Christian Fellowship; appointed as "Fellow of the Most

Excellent Order of International Experts (FOIE)" in the field of Entrepreneurship.

- Received Honorary Doctorate Degree in Philosophy from CICA International University & Seminary.
- Became an Amazon Best-Selling Author with my book, *STOP Asking for Permission & Give Notice.*
- Brand advertised in a digital marketing billboard campaign in Times Square– Manhattan, NY.
- Released book, *2018 Legacy Journal & Planner: A Planning Tool for your Freedom & Future.*
- Served as a Rise and Grind Ambassador for Shark Tank's Daymond John's newest book, *Rise and Grind.*

2018

- Theatrical production *Get Out of Your Own Way* premieres in Hollywood, CA.
- Released book, *I Want To Quit My Job.: 8 Entrepreneurial Strategies For Massive Results While Employed.*
- Released two book anthologies, *Bruised, Broken & Blessed & "Get Out of Your Own Way"*
- Studied under NAACP Image Award-winning author Victoria Christopher Murray.
- Featured Author at the 2018 NAACP National Convention & Panelist
- Pen Legacy officially trademarked and registered as an official business in Montgomery County, PA.

2019

- Theatrical production Get Out of Your Own Way completed an encore performance in Hollywood, CA.& premiere on 42nd St in Manhattan, NY
- Compiled & Published two book anthologies, "*Get Out of Your Own Way*" Vol 2 & Vol. 3
- Released two books, *Fear Is A Crime and Secure Your Legacy Journal*
- Received a Certificate of Recognition from Jersey City Mayor Steven M. Fulop, a Senate Citation from the Senate of New Jersey, a New Jersey General Assembly Resolution, and Office of the Hudson County Executive Citation. (picture above w/ Assemblywoman Angela V. McKnight (D-NJ)

2020

- Compiled book anthology: Slay Your Legacy: 9 Keys to Manifesting The Life You Want
- Press Features on NBC, CBS, FOX & iWorship96 Radio
- Released books, When Shift Happens: 21 Days of Celebrating the Lessons of Life & Detours & Michelle and Her Magical Pen
- Secured training with Shark Tank's Daymond John & Celebrity PR Agent Monique Jackson
- Pen Legacy officially registered as a business in the State of Florida

2021

- Press Feature Interview / Cover with Fashion GXD Magazine
- Featured Press with Amazon Live, The Blueprint Live, K.I.S. H Magazine (Fall 2021), Medium.com, BlackNews.com, 21st Century Authors, Kidlio Magazine & RollingOut Magazine
- Interviewed alongside TV/Radio Cathy Hughes of TV One on The Madison Jaye Show (streaming on Pandora, iHeart Radio, & Spotify)
- Featured Writer in two editions of FlightInStilettos Magazine
- Released six children's books: Imagine Life Without African American Inventors, Michelle Goes To Paris, Michelle Goes to Congress, Michelle Goes To The Beach, Michelle Sells No Books
- Partnered with Flights In Stilettos, LLC to release Michelle Goes To The Beach Microfiber Beach Towel
- Joined Ms. Evelyn Braxton's book team and became her official Author Agent for the book "Cooking With Ms. E"
- Submitted books "Imagine Life Without African-American Inventors" & "Michelle Goes to Congress" for nomination in the category of "Outstanding Literary Work - Children" with the 53rd NAACP Image Awards
- Nominated for Best Children's Book with the B.A.R. Literary Awards in New Orleans, LA.

2022

- Participated in a Virtual Book Tour with the African Americans on the Move Book Club for the month of February promoting her book. "Imagine Life Without African-American Inventors".
- The Adventure of Michelle Book Series was placed in the Wilmington Library and North Wilmington Library in Delaware.
- The Rochdale Village Community Center in Jamacia, NY, honored Charron Monaye as their Author of the Month. They purchased 30 books for the community center and hosted a virtual reading event where Charron Monaye read to the children.
- Ms. Monaye appeared on Style w/ Trysh" Show (Season 2, Ep. 2. Aired on April 10, 2022) where she was interviewed.
- Featured Press with Black & Published, Today's Purpose Woman, & ShoutOut Atlanta
- Ms. Monaye's books and brand were advertised on digital billboards in Atlanta, Las Vegas, Memphis, and Los Angeles.
- Released a new book under the "Adventures of Michelle Book Series," Michelle Opens Her First Bank Account

THE
CHARRON MONAYE
COLLECTION

POETRY • CHILDREN'S • BUSINESS • JOURNALING
DEVOTIONAL • NON-FICTION • PERSONAL DEVELOPMENT • BOOK ANTHOLOGIES

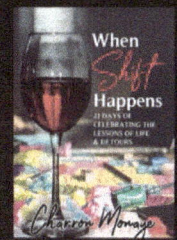

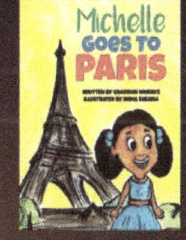

Table of Contents

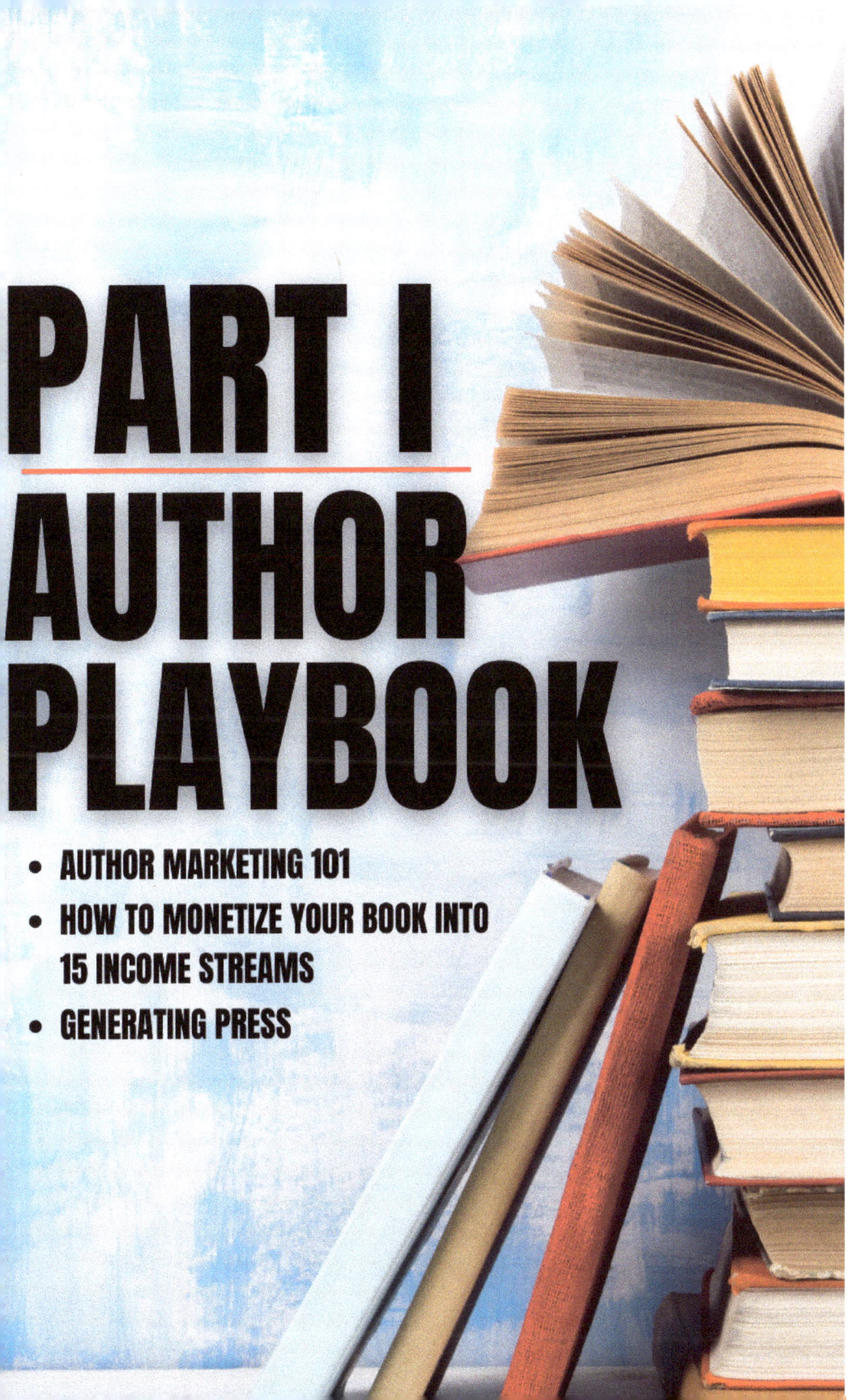

PART I
AUTHOR
PLAYBOOK

- **AUTHOR MARKETING 101**
- **HOW TO MONETIZE YOUR BOOK INTO 15 INCOME STREAMS**
- **GENERATING PRESS**

Author Marketing 101

Marketing refers to all activities a company does to promote and sell products or services to consumers. At its core, marketing seeks to take a product or service, identify its ideal customers, and draw the customers' attention to the product or service available. Marketing makes use of the "marketing mix," also known as the six Ps—product, price, place, promotion, process, and physical evidence.

Product ~ the products or services a business is offering.

- Price ~ the entire pricing methodology for products or services, and how customers will react to it.
- Promotion ~ the act of marketing directly to consumers.
- Place ~ You need to ensure that customers can find your product or service with ease.
- Process ~ The delivery of your product or service to a customer.
- Physical evidence ~ Your consumer should always receive something physical to validate their purchase.

The Marketing Plan

A marketing plan is a strategic roadmap that businesses use to organize, execute, and track their marketing strategy over a given time period.

Step 1: Take a snapshot of your company's current situation.

_____

_____

_____

Step 2: Define who your target audience is.

_____

_____

_____

Step 3: Make a list of your marketing goals.

_____

_____

_____

Step 4: Research marketing tactics.

_____

_____

_____

Step 5: Set your marketing budget.

_____

_____

_____

Author Branding

A brand is a **consistent promise to a customer** about what they are going to get, in terms of product quality, customer service and more, and how what they get will be different from the competition.

7 ways to build your author brand

Identify your reader ~ Who is it that will align best with the books you write and who is most likely to buy?

_____

_____

_____

Develop your brand voice ~ How do you want others to see you? What do you want people to think when they hear your name?

_____

_____

_____

Figure out your USP ~ Knowing your USP, or unique selling point, is essential if you want to get across to readers why they should buy your books. How are you different?

_____

_____

_____

Set some expectations ~ The aim of your brand is to tell your readers what they can expect from you. When you are consistent it helps people to get to know, like and trust you, which is essential when growing an author platform.

_____

_____

_____

Know what you're branding ~ The key is to brand you, not your book. This is particularly important to remember if you are writing your first book.

_____

_____

_____

Choose a look ~ It's the color palette, graphics and visual cues, photos and typeface. Yes, it's also the logo!

Apply your brand everywhere ~ Your brand is made up of everything you do and say, so you should consciously implement it everywhere – your social channels, promotional bookmarks or business cards, even your email signature.

Author Advertising

Newspaper ~ can promote your business to a wide range of customers. Display advertisements are placed throughout the paper, while classified listings are under subject headings in a specific section.

Magazine ~ Magazines generally serve consumers (by interest group e.g., women) and trade (industry/business type e.g., hospitality).

Radio ~ Advertising on the radio is a great way to reach your target audience. If your target market listens to a particular station, then regular advertising can attract new customers.

Television ~ Television has an extensive reach and advertising this way is ideal if you cater to a large market in a large area.

Directories ~ Directories list businesses by name or category (e.g., Yellow Pages phone directories). Customers who refer to directories have often already made up their mind to buy - they just need to decide who to buy from.

Outdoor and transit ~ Outdoor billboards can be signs by the road or hoardings at sport stadiums. Transit advertising can be posters on buses, taxis and bicycles. Large billboards can get your message across with a big impact.

Direct mail, catalogues and leaflets ~ Direct mail means writing to customers directly. The more precise your mailing list or distribution area, the more of your target market you will reach.

Online ~ A well-designed website can entice customers to buy from you. There are a number of ways you can promote your business online via paid advertising or to improve your search engine rankings.

Let's Increase Book Sales

Realize that marketing doesn't stop once the book is distributed. It truly just begins!!!!

☐ Does your book synopsis explain, "Why should someone buy your book? What's in it for them? If they're going to be paying you money, they often want to ensure they're getting their money's worth."

☐ Get book reviews

☐ Create ads

☐ Host a book launch event or party (in-person or virtual)

☐ Research the market to place your book within the right book category.

☐ Know the trending keywords in order to make your book discoverable

☐ Upgrade your Author Bio ~ Do you sound appealing as a person

☐ Get Book Endorsements

☐ Secure and leverage press

☐ Be consistent with Marketing, Branding, and

Advertising

How to Become a #1 Best-Selling Author on Amazon

Every book has an Amazon best-sellers rank. Number 1 is the current best-selling book on amazon and #4,959,688 is the worst-selling book. Amazon updates their sales rankings every hour based on an algorithm that counts total sales of all books for the last 30 days. Every. Single. Hour.

All book rankings on Amazon are relative. That means it is not just about hitting a specific number of sales; you have to sell more books than the competition in a given period of time to outrank them.

Here are a few steps to make your journey helpful:

Step 1: Find best-seller categories

_____

_____

_____

Step 2: Analyze the Competition

_____

_____

_____

Step 2A: Design a great cover

(What is your book cover vision?)

_____

_____

_____

Step 2B: Find engaging keywords

_____

_____

_____

Step 2C: Hook your readers with a great opening

_____

_____

_____

Step 2D: Listen to the readers in your market

_____

_____

_____

Step 3: Know how many sales you need to hit #1 in each category. (You can do that with our Amazon Book Sales Calculator.

https://www.tckpublishing.com/amazon-book-sales-calculator/

_____

_____

_____

Step 4: Choose your 2 target categories

_____

_____

Step 5: Get Amazon to list your book in your ideal categories

_____

_____

_____

How to Become a #1 New York Times Best-Selling Author

If you want a realistic shot to become a bestseller, you must sell at least 5,000 – 10,000 copies in one week. The necessary amount fluctuates based on the level of competition and the number of new releases during each week. The non-fiction lists tend to be more competitive and usually require weekly sales of 7,500 copies or more. The New York Times counts weekly sales starting the previous Sunday through Saturday.

The New York Times requires that book sales be spread across America using multiple retailers, including Amazon, B&N bookstores, Books-a-Million, independent bookstores, etc. Sales must be dispersed, rather than concentrated.

Below are the names and number of available slots for each type of adult book list:

- Fiction Combined Print & E-Book List – 15 total slots

- Fiction Hardcover List – 15 total slots

- Fiction Paperback List – 10 total slots

- Non-Fiction Combined Print & E-Book List – 15 total slots
- Non-Fiction Hardcover List – 15 total slots
- Non-Fiction Paperback List – 10 total slots
- Non-Fiction Advice, How-To & Miscellaneous List – 10 total slots
- 3 Non-Fiction Monthly Lists: Business, Science, and Sports – 10 total slots

Monetize Your Book Into 15 Income Streams

- Sell A Video Course

- Start A Non-Profit

- Start A Publishing Company

- Start a Summer Camp

- Create a Podcast

- Become a Blog writer

- Create a weekend conference/retreat

- Create A Coaching/Mastermind

- Ghostwriting

- Create an app or sell software

- Play Script (Film it for distribution)

- Paid speaking engagements

- Create a membership group

- Adapt your book into different languages

- Host workshops

Understand The Power of Monetization

- Merchandise
- T-Shirts
- Mugs
- Bags
- Notepads & Pens
- Workbooks

Generating Press

Types of Press

- Radio / Blog talk/ Podcast
- TV / News Outlets
- Magazines / Newspaper/ Flyers

Items Needs When Pitching

- (EPK)
- Target PitchList
- Press Release
- Media Alert

Target Pitch List

Find Your Audience. Use your audience geographic, demographics, and psychographics to make a list of media outlets they are tuned into.

_____

_____

_____

_____

Do your research and find journalists and show hosts from those media outlets who cover topics within your niche.

_____

_____

_____

_____

Build relationships, before you pitch!

- Do your research and be familiar with the types or articles or interviews the journalist or hosts does.
- Send the journalist/host an email complimenting a recent article or interview.
- Be genuine and make sure it relevant to your niche or a shared interest. Share content with the journalist/host like articles, videos, reports, etc.

CHARRON MONAYE

Press Release

First Paragraph: The 5 W's (who, what, when, where, why), and the how: Begin with the most important and captivating information. Be clear and concise. Describe and explain why the topic is vital or interesting.

Body Paragraphs: The next two paragraphs (usually 2-3) are meant to support the first paragraph. Quotes, background information and a full company description can be included.

Call to Action (CTA): What do you want your targeted audience to do? Provide a concise direction of what you want your audience to do. For example, a freebie, free trial, include a link to click to follow on social media channels or to subscribe to your blog, etc.

Boilerplate: The boilerplate describes what your business does and is usually the last paragraph of your press release. You can usually reuse it at the end of all of your business press releases.

End Notation: Typically, the end of a press release is noted with "###" - historically, it would indicate to the printer that it is the end of the press release, but now it has simply become customary.

Media Alert

What's a media alert?

A media alert is an invitation sent out to the media to a company event, presentation, news conference or grand opening. It is meant to generate interest without giving way the story.

What's the difference between a media alert & press release?

As mentioned above, a media alert announces or invites the media to something that is happening. On the other hand, a press release gives all of the details about the company event, presentation, news conference or grand opening.

Key Tips To Getting Press

Getting publicity is a series of steps that you can simply repeat, and you'll get the same or similar results time and time again. Follow these steps below and see it happen

Know Your Audience, Their Struggles and How You Can Help Them Overcome Them. Simple as that.

_____

_____

_____

Know Your Business' Strength(s). What makes your company different than others in the market?

_____

_____

_____

Know Your Objective(s). You MUST know your desired outcome(s) and be able to state it clearly.

_____

_____

_____

Determine Your Target Media Audience. Make a list of online media, TV and radio programs, and newspapers that are in your area of expertise.

_____

_____

_____

Have An Angle. What about your service(s) or product(s) is compelling, will make your audience curious, or is controversial?

_____

_____

_____

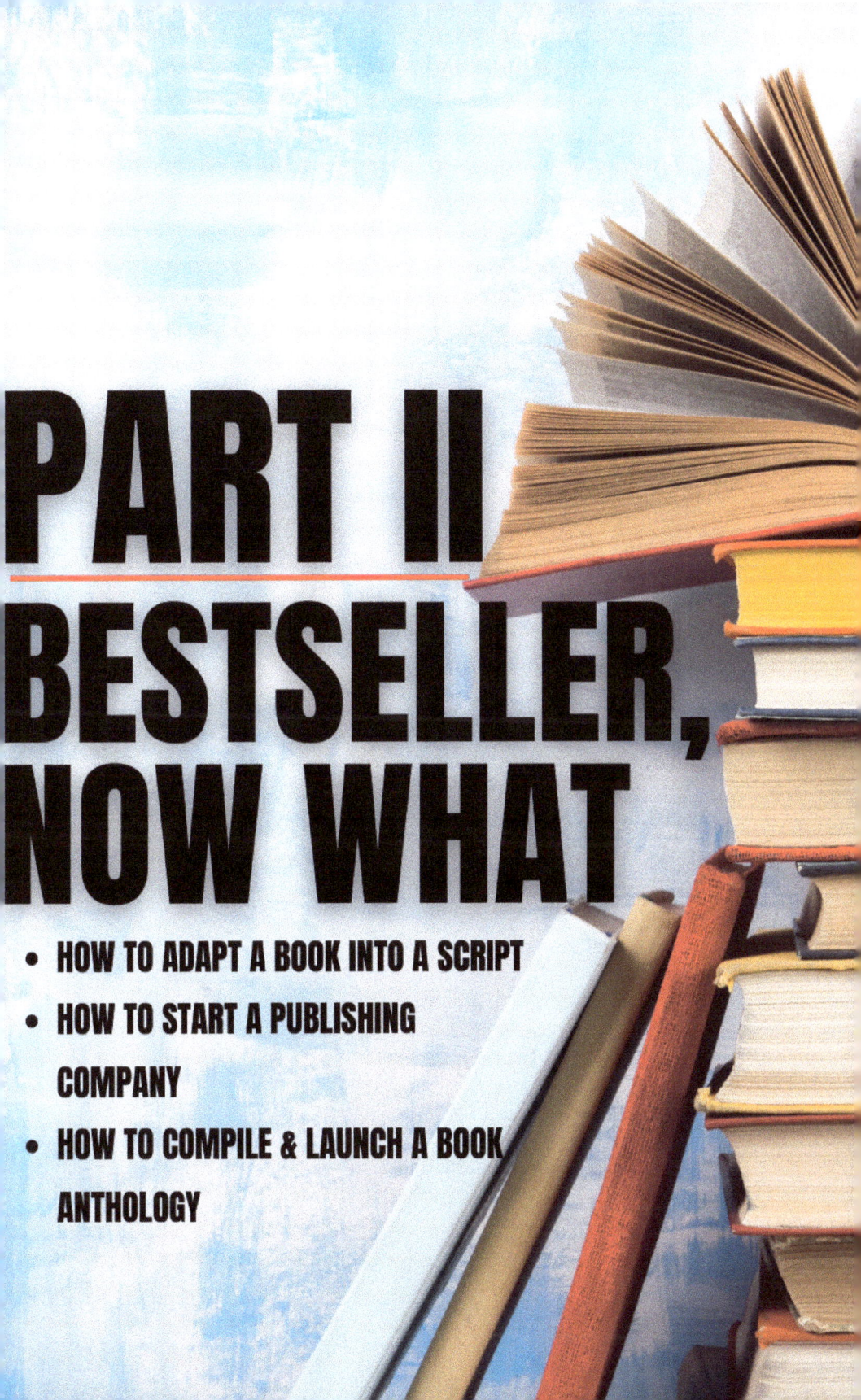

PART II

BESTSELLER, NOW WHAT

- HOW TO ADAPT A BOOK INTO A SCRIPT
- HOW TO START A PUBLISHING COMPANY
- HOW TO COMPILE & LAUNCH A BOOK ANTHOLOGY

How To Adapt A Book Into A Script

Types of Script

- Playscript ~ a script used in a theater production

- Teleplay ~ A teleplay is a screenplay or script used in the production of a scripted television program or series.

- Screenplay ~ A screenplay, or script, is a written work by screenwriters for a film, television program or video game.

Elements of a Play Script

There are seven basic formatting elements that make up the text pages of a properly formatted playscript. These are

- Page Numbering

- Act/Scene designations

- The Setting description

- Blackout/Curtain/End designations

- Character Names

- Dialogue, and

- Stage Directions

Teleplay

- Generally speaking, hour long episode scripts can be anywhere from 45-63 pages, although a majority of the time you want to stick with 50-55 pages. The basic sense of it is that one-page equals one minute, and with a sixty-minute show, you obviously need to account for commercial breaks.

- Sitcoms, minus the commercials, are typically 22 minutes long. Thus, a sitcom script is generally between 25 and 40 pages long. Every sitcom episode has a main plot (story A), as well as one or two subplots (B & C stories).

Screenplay

In the most basic terms, a screenplay is a 90–120-page document written in Courier 12pt font on 8 1/2" x 11" bright white three-hole punched paper.

One formatted script page in Courier font equals roughly one minute of screen time. The elements for a script are:

- Scene Heading.

- Action.

- Character Name.

- Dialogue.

- Parenthetical.

- Extensions.

- Transition.

- Shot.

Adapting a Book into a Script

- ☐ Adaption of Book To Script
- ☐ Decide If It Would Make a Good Movie
- ☐ Read Screenwriting Books
- ☐ Read Professional Scripts
- ☐ Write Outlines of Movies
- ☐ Write Out Your Novel As an Outline
- ☐ Zero in on Your Movie's Main Conflict
- ☐ Turn Your Novel Outline Into a Script Outline
- ☐ Buy Some Screenwriting Software
- ☐ Begin Writing Your Script
- ☐ Get Feedback on your Screenplay and Rewrite

Production Team (Theater)

Pre-Production

- Producer
- Director
- Playwright
- Set designer
- Lighting designer
- Costume designer
- Sound designer
- Music director

Production

- Actor
- Carpenter and master carpenter
- Front of house manager
- Playbill writer
- Publicist
- Stage manager
- Technical director
- Stagehands

- Wardrobe supervisor

Production Team (Movie)

- Producer

- Director

- Screenwriter

- Production Designer

- Art Designer

- Costume Designer

- Actors

- Music Supervisor

- Cinematographer (DP)

- Editor

3 Steps To Market Your Script

STEP 1. Write a great script – Intriguing concept, cool characters, and well written.

- Keep rewriting that script until it is a showpiece. The more you can establish a reputation of you being a professional, the better your chance of success. Remember, every page of your script either says you are an amateur or a Pro. So, make them the best they can be.

STEP 2. Use your writing skills to create a compelling pitch.

- If you can say your pitch in one or two interesting sentences, you've tripled your chance of success. Make sure it is concise, has a hook that intrigues us, and has us see the story in our mind.

STEP 3. Connect to get your script to a "Champion."

- You've got a great script, a great pitch, and now you need it in the hands of a champion – someone with connections. Your champion might be a producer, agent, manager, or a friend on the inside. You just need to find someone who loves your writing and can't stop themselves from promoting it.

Screenplay Elements

Scene Heading

- Indent: Left: 0.0" Right: 0.0" Width: 6.0"

- A scene heading is a one-line description of the location and time of day of a scene, also known as a "slugline." It should always be in CAPS.

- Example: EXT. WRITERS STORE - DAY reveals that the action takes place outside The Writers Store during the daytime.

Sub header

- Indent: Left: 0.0" Right: 0.0" Width: 6.0"

When a new scene heading is not necessary, but some distinction needs to be made in the action, you can use a sub header. But be sure to use these sparingly, as a script full of sub headers is generally frowned upon. A good example is when there are a series of quick cuts between two locations, you would use the term INTERCUT and the scene locations

Action ~ Indent: Left: 0.0" Right: 0.0" Width: 6.0"

The narrative description of the events of a scene, written in the present tense. Also less commonly known as direction, visual exposition, black stuff, description or scene direction.

Character ~ Indent: Left: 2.0" Right: 0.0" Width: 4.0"

When a character is introduced, his name should be capitalized within the action. For example: The door opens and in walks LIAM, a thirty-something hipster with attitude to spare.
A character's name is CAPPED and always listed above his lines of dialogue. Minor characters may be listed without names, for example "TAXI DRIVER" or "CUSTOMER."

Dialogue ~ Indent: Left: 1.0" Right: 1.5" Width: 3.5"

Lines of speech for each character. Dialogue format is used anytime a character is heard speaking, even for off-screen and voice-over.

Shot ~ Indent: Left: 0.0" Right: 0.0" Width: 6.0"

A shot tells the reader the focal point within a scene has changed. Like a transition, there's rarely a time when a spec screenwriter should insert shot directions. Once again, that's the director's job.
Examples of Shots:
- ANGLE ON --
- EXTREME CLOSE UP --
- PAN TO --
- LIAM'S POV --

Parenthetical ~ Indent: Left: 1.5" Right: 2.0" Width: 2.5"

A parenthetical is direction for the character, which is either attitude or action oriented.

Extension

Placed after the character's name, in parentheses. An abbreviated technical note placed after the character's name to indicate how the voice will be heard onscreen, for example, if the character is speaking as a voice-over, it would appear as LIAM (V.O.).

Transition ~ Indent: Left: 4.0" Right: 0.0" Width: 2.0"

Transitions are film editing instructions, and generally only appear in a shooting script. Transition verbiage includes:
- CUT TO:
- DISSOLVE TO:
- SMASH CUT:
- QUICK CUT:
- FADE TO:

Spec Script vs. Shooting Script

A **"spec script"** literally means that you are writing a screenplay on speculation. That is, no one is paying you to write the script. You are penning it in hopes of selling the script to a buyer. Spec scripts should stick stringently to established screenwriting rules.

Once a script is purchased, it becomes a **shooting script**, also called a production script. This is a version of the screenplay created for film production. It will include technical instructions, like film editing notes, shots, cuts and the like. All the scenes are numbered, and revisions are marked with a color-coded system. This is done so that the production assistants and director can then arrange the order in which the scenes will be shot for the most efficient use of stage, cast, and location resources.

FYI: A spec script should NEVER contain the elements of shooting script. The biggest mistake any new screenwriter can make is to submit a script full of production language, including camera angles and editing transitions. It can be very difficult to resist putting this type of language in your script. After all, it's your story and you see it in a very specific way. However, facts are facts. If you want to direct your script, then try to go the independent filmmaker route. But if you want to sell your script, then stick to the accepted spec screenplay format.

Gaining Exposure For Your Book As A Playwright

- Leverage your Script as a Product of the book

- Network with other authors and playwrights in the cities you wish to enter.

- Host Book Signings

- Secure Radio and Print Coverage

- Go Visit & Support Other Productions

- Use Social Media as a Networking Event

- Partner with another author/playwright to learn from and use their brand to leverage yours.

- Travel, Socialize, Sell, and Repeat

The Steps to Starting a Publishing Company

What is Book Publishing?

- Publishing is the dissemination of literature, music, or information. It is the activity of making information available to the general public.

- Publishing includes the following stages of development: acquisition, copy editing, production, printing (and its electronic equivalents), marketing, and distribution.

4 Types of Publishing

- **Traditional book publishing is** when a publisher offers the author a contract and, in turn, prints, publishes, and sells your book through booksellers and other retailers. The publisher essentially buys the right to publish your book and pays you royalties from the sales.

- **Vanity book publishing** ~ A vanity press, vanity publisher, or subsidy publisher is a publishing house in which authors pay to have their books published. The publisher will offer publishing services or packages that the client can choose. This form of publishing has both elements of self-publishing and traditional publishing because the author is technically still being published through self-publishing methods, and even though you pay for the services, some companies will take royalties from your sells.

- **A small press** is an independent publishing house that has a fully staffed publishing team – think editors, proofreaders, designers, and typesetters – but runs a smaller operation than the big-name publishers.

  Benefits:

  - Increased involvement: Because a small press is working with fewer authors, small-press authors have a hand in decisions that are often withheld from authors signed on with bigger publishers.

  - More freedom: Because they're independent, small-press publishers have greater freedom, a willingness to think outside the box, and are sometimes more open-minded about publishing and marketing decisions.

  - Faster turnaround: Because they're juggling fewer projects, it's common for small-scale operations to provide quicker turnaround times, getting the book to print faster.

- Eligible for awards: Small presses often submit their books for literary prizes and awards for which self-published authors aren't eligible.

- **Self-Publishing** is when the author controls the entire process, including design, price, distribution, marketing, and public relations. The author may perform these activities themselves or they may outsource these tasks.

  - In traditional publishing, the publisher bears the costs, such as editing, marketing, and paying advances, and reaps a substantial share of the profits; by comparison, in self-publishing, the author bears all of these costs but earns a higher share of the profit.

Some of the Biggest Differences

- **Traditional** ~ Sell Over Your Rights, For Royalties, but get better marketing, in stores, and publicity

- **Self-Publishing** ~ Keep Your Rights, Do & Pay For All of the Work, but no help with promotion, not available in stores and pay $$ for publicist

- **Vanity** ~ Keep Your Right, Pay for Publishing Services, but no support or assistance afterwards.

How To Create An
Indie Publishing Company

☐ Create a Name

☐ Connect To Your Already Established Business, or Because you will make over $600, you must make this a Business (LLC is preferred)

☐ Get EIN Number

☐ Build A Team

☐ Create Publishing Package

☐ Generate a Marketing Strategy

☐ Create an account through Bowker (ISBN Distributor)

☐ Purchase ISBN #'s & Barcodes to have ready to use

☐ Search and Select your Distribution Company

Services To Offer

- ☐ Book cover design

- ☐ Interior layout / Typeset

- ☐ Marketing Materials (Flyers, Bookmarks)

- ☐ Barcode & ISBN

- ☐ Coaching Sessions

- ☐ Marketing Plan

- ☐ Paperback & eBook Online Distribution

- ☐ Free Complimentary Books (Always give them an inventory to start with)

The Power of Pre-sales

Pre-order sales are important for two reasons.

First, publishers use pre-orders as leverage to convince retailers to stock up early on a new book. Filling the distribution pipeline before the launch date is crucial to maximize sales and boost the bestseller potential. If distribution is weak and availability runs out then a book can get listed as "out of stock," which can ruin all hopes of hitting a bestseller list.

Second, there's a secret about pre-orders that many authors don't know. The New York Times allows all pre-orders to be counted towards a book's first week of sales.

Distribution

The most important thing to know about distribution is that more than half of all book sales (regardless of format) take place online. Therefore, your job is to create a connection for either eBook, Print Book (Paperback or Hardback) and/or Audible.

Book Distributors:

- Amazon Kindle Publishing (KDP)
- Lightning Source
- Ingram Sparks
- Independent Publisher Group
- Baker & Taylor
- Publishers Group West

ISBN Numbers & Barcode

The International Standard Book Number is a numeric commercial book identifier which is intended to be unique. Publishers purchase ISBNs from an affiliate of the International ISBN Agency. An ISBN is assigned to each edition and variation of a book.

The most visually recognizable, the UPC (Universal Product Code) is a linear 1D barcode made up of two parts: the barcode and the 12-digit UPC number. The first six numbers of the barcode is the manufacturer's identification number. The next five digits represent the item's number.

Library of Congress Submission

A Library of Congress catalog control number is a unique identification number that the Library of Congress assigns to the catalog record created for each book in its cataloged collections. Librarians use it to locate a specific Library of Congress catalog record in the national databases and to order catalog cards from the Library of Congress or from commercial suppliers. The purpose of the Preassigned Control Number (PCN) program is to enable the Library of Congress to assign control numbers in advance of publication to those titles that may be added to the Library's collections.

Website: https://www.loc.gov/publish/pcn/

How to Compile & Launch A Book Anthology

What Is A Book Anthology?

- An anthology is a collection of short pieces, usually written by *other people* than the "editor" (author) of the collection itself.

Co-Author vs Author

Co-Author

- Contributes significantly to the conception, design, execution, and/or analysis and interpretation of data

- Participates in drafting and/or revising part of the manuscript for intellectual content

- Approves of the version to be published

- Agrees to be accountable for all aspects of the work

Author

- Is the creator or originator of any written work such as a book or play and is thus also a writer. More broadly defined, an author is "the person who originated or gave existence to anything" and whose authorship determines responsibility for what was created.[

Author vs. Compiler

Author

- Is the creator or originator of any written work such as a book or play and is thus also a writer. More broadly defined, an author is "the person who originated or gave existence to anything" and whose authorship determines responsibility for what was created.

Compiler

- Is a person who facilitates the process of bringing together writers to publish an anthology. The compiler is the author of the book and is usually the company that holds all publishing rights.

The Benefits of Co-Author Books

- You help people share their story without having the full cost of publishing a full book.

- You serve as an expert and leader in a project.

- You offer people an opportunity to develop a product they can add to their brand or use to leverage their business.

- It can serve as an income stream for you.

- It's a great marketing tool, which gives your company, business exposure.

- It's a product that shows your ability to give back and help others live out their dreams

Disadvantages of Co-Authoring

- You are the facilitator and MUST know the ins and outs of publishing and the book world.

- The co-authors hold no publishing right to the book and must sale the book as a part of their brand to earn money.

- You must deal with a lot of personalities, and attitudes. You took their money, and they demand a business, yet fun process.

- Once the book is launched, the life and legacy of the book belongs to all of you as a group.

- If not used correctly, co-author books can serve as a negative process for individuals and can tarnish your brand as a whole

What is the Business of Book Anthologies?

As Compiler, what is your role:

- Provide detailed and concrete details of expectations
- Providing agreements / contracts
- Provide a clear calendar of deadlines on all areas
- Determine the Book Retailer Price and Book Details
- Have a clear theme and/or topic for them to write on
- How will they get paid?

You should get everything in writing because this will be a true partnership in every sense of the word. Don't rely on friendship to carry you through lawsuits.

- Who will hold the copyright?

- Who will apply for the ISBN?

- How will costs be divided?

- What Are You Offer?

- How will income from book sales be divided?

- How will speaking engagements that result be assigned? (You will probably get calls for speaking as a result of a good book. How will those requests be divided if both parties are speakers?)

- Will the book be paperback or hardbound? How many pages? How will we decide on a cover design & graphics? Who will write what?

All of these need to be agreed-upon before starting.

Slay Your Legacy

CHARRON MONA

TONI MOORE ESQ.

BARBARA ALLEN

KINYATTA E. GRAY

KIAWANA LEAF

KEISHA GRIFFIN

ANDREL HARRIS

TERALEEN CAMPBELL

TINESHA BOSWELL

ONTARIA KIM WILSON

Marketing A Co-Author Book

- Promote, Promote, Promote

- Network with other Readers and Writers, Book Signings are your friend

- Enjoy Pre-Sales, they are your friend!

- Create a marketing plan for your team.

- Make Marketing A Requirement for your Team

- Create Marketing Materials for your Co-Authors

Launch To Bestseller

Ensure

- Ensure All Co-Authors have received their products, and all obligations are done.

Communicate

- Communicate all selling opportunities out there that they can do as a team, or individuals

Provide

- Provide details on how to brand their books into their own personal businesses.

Offer

- Offer them the opportunity to publish their full story with you, by offering them a discount. The goal is not to keep them co-authors but help them elevate their stories into a legacy

Give

- Give them a survey to complete to obtain feedback on their experience. It is always better to hear how you did from them rather than on social media!

Tell

- Tell them how they can order more book from you, and always keep the lines of communication open!

Publishing For Profits Checklist

The purpose of this checklist is to give both new and seasoned authors an at-a-glance gauge of the publishing for profits process of any book.

It must be acknowledged that book development is a creative process and that quality can be subjective. To meet professional standards, any book should be grammatically accurate and free of spelling and typographical errors, categorized correctly, priced accordingly, and marketable to readers, press, and publishers, and/or film makers. This checklist is broken into two sections: (1) Pre-Publishing, (2) Publishing and (3) Post Publishing

Even though this checklist can was created for the self-publisher in mind, it is also suitable for any author who decides to go with an Indie, Vanity, or Traditional Publisher. Please note: if you do hire a publishing service company to do the publishing for you, everything pertaining to the book creation and distribution will be done by them, and you will just focus on the other items. In order to publish for profits, all writers should know what steps they should take to maximize profit potential and gain massive exposure.

Pre-Publishing

- Determine Your Book Need In The Marketplace
- Research & Finalize Your Book Title & Book Synopsis
- Figure out Your Book Messaging for Your Cover Design
- Determine Your Ideal Reader & Audience
- Research & Plan Your Market & Press Strategy
- Determine Your Distribution Platform (Publish or Print)
- Hire A Ghostwriter or Writing Coach
- Write Your Compelling, yet Relatable Story
- Determine Your Publishing Method (Self-Indie, Vanity, or traditional)
- Hire A Marketable Designer to Create Your Book Cover
- Hire A Professional Editor (developmentally edited, copyedited, and proofread)
- Hire A Book Typesetter/Formatter
- Purchase IBSN and Barcode
- Establish & Execute Your Author Platform Through Branding & Marketing
- Research The Marketplace to Properly Categorize Your Book

Publishing Process

- Book Cover Completed
- Editing, Rewrites, and Final Editing Is Completed
- Manuscript is Converted Into Distribution Book Files (.pdf for paperback covers and interior & .epub., .rtf., word.; .mobi for e-book, and .mp3 or .aac for audio)
- Research The Marketplace To Determine Book Prices
- Determine Your Trim Size & Book Categories
- Set-Up Book Distribution & Execute Marketing and Advertising
- Solicit Pre-Sales through Your Various Book Retailers
- Create and Submit Your Press Release (2 – 4 weeks prior)
- Connect to Book Clubs for Placement
- Solicit Press & Media to Secure Interviews / Publicity
- Plan Your Book Release Celebration
- Research Events & Book Fairs to Participate
- Copyright Your Final Manuscript After Editing
- Submit Files to Distributor or Printer for Manuscript to Book Conversion
- Submit Copies to Influencers &/or Beta Readers to Guarantee Reviews

Post Publishing (After Distribution)

- Attend & Collaborate in Book Signings
- Execute your Press List and Solicit Media Coverage
- Bundle Your Book
- Convert Your Book Into 15 Income Streams
- Solicit Reviews on Book Retailer Sites
- Collaborate With Other Authors to Maximize Exposure
- Adapt Your Book Into Other Languages or Formats

I know many of you are thinking, Charron, I don't know how to do half of this! Welp, this could be why your book is not profitable. As I teach me author masterminds and publishing clients, publishing is more than just uploading some files and sharing on social media. ***Are you publishing for popularity or profit?***

About The Author

From a struggling mother to Amazon best-selling author, Charron Monaye is an adored storyteller and groundbreaking writing expert who has evolved into a Who's Who in America's Arts and Literature. With over twenty-five years in the industry, Charron has been recognized, nationally and internationally, as a literary game-changer who does not mind adapting words into legacies.

Dedicated to facilitating the growth and evolution of individuals ready to win, Charron has contributed her pen to the literary industry for over two decades. Her body of works includes over twenty published books in six different genres, five Amazon best-sellers (with six-figure sales and winner of various awards), staff writer for CNN iReport and Philadelphia Association of Paralegals, contributing author for 20+ book publications, celebrity ghostwriter, award-winning playwright, blogger, editor-in-chief of madisonjaye.com, and creator/writer of five stage performances. Her stage play, *Get Out of Your Own Way*, is her most successful play, to date, with premieres and sold-out audiences in Hollywood, CA and Times Square, NY. She has also been featured in several major press publications, including CBS, NBC, FOX, *Sheen Magazine*, *Philadelphia Tribune*, *Huff Post*, *Vine Magazine*, and *DivaGoals Daily*, to name a few.

A woman of passion, vision, and purpose, Charron embodies a no-nonsense approach in her message and teaching style. Transparent, truthful, and wise, she is a living testament to the value of "Loving the Real You" and the power in knowing how to "Stop Asking for Permission & Give Notice." Charron uses real-life solutions and straight talk to deliver her consistent message of speaking to teach, living your best life, and the importance of building a wealthy legacy.

Today, Charron is the founder of Pen Legacy, LLC. This groundbreaking literary company helps individuals share their stories and provides a platform to elevate their voices through book publishing, literary coaching, and the adaptation of books into scripts. From its inception in 2015, Pen Legacy, LLC. has published 100+ books, with more than half becoming Amazon Bestsellers. In addition, Charron Monaye is the mastermind and author coach behind the author careers of Ms. Evelyn Braxton (Braxton Family Values), Precious L. Williams, Esq. (13x Pitch Champion), Ty Johnston-Chavis (TV/Film Producer & Pitch Coach), just to name a few.

Charron has a Bachelor of Arts in Political Science from West Chester University, a Master's in Public Administration from Keller Graduate School of Management, a Certificate in Paralegal Studies and Life Coaching, and a Doctor of Philosophy (Humane Letters) from CICA International University & Seminary. She was also appointed as "Fellow of the Most Excellent Order of International Experts (FOIE)" in the field of entrepreneurship from the United Nations and has been awarded and recognized for her work as an author, book publisher, and playwright.

Charron is a member of Zeta Phi Beta Sorority, Inc., Order of Eastern Star and First Baptist Church of Crestmont. She resides in Wesley Chapel, Florida, and is the proud mother of two sons, Christopher and Craig.